From a Mess to a Message

Anna Marie McCutchen

Edited by Anthony Ambrogio

Cover Design by Brittany J. Jackson

Published by G Publishing LLC

Library of Congress Control Number: 2011945046

ISBN: 978-0-9849360-0-7

Printed in the United States of America

Dedication

This book is dedicated to my dear, loving mother Carolyn Elizabeth McCutchen, who, through much discipline and chastisement, helped to shape my life in a positive way. I would venture to say that any loving parent should train his or her child in a disciplined manner. When the child comes of age, he or she will give honor. Proverbs 22:6: "Train up a child in the way he should go, and, when he is old, he will never depart from it."

The purpose of this book is to encourage and uplift every reader that it reaches—to get readers to realize that, no matter how messy their lives may have been, God can turn them around in a way that will work in his favor. Psalm 30:5 NKJV: "For his anger is but for a moment; his favor is for life; weeping may endure for a night, but joy comes in the morning."

"Look back and thank God. Look forward and trust God. Look around and serve God. Look within and find God. God closes doors no man can open, and opens doors no man can close."—Anonymous

Table of Contents

Chapter 1: Testimony

We overcome the world by the word of our testimony and by the blood of Jesus Christ (Rev 12:11). But, often, we keep ourselves closed up.

If we must be closed up, we should be closed up not like a clam but like a cocoon; we should anticipate change—we should *long* for it.

It's time today to transform from a caterpillar to a butterfly. We need to share our testimony. To bring hope to others who thought they would never make it because of all the turmoil in their lives.

This realization might be painful, but, when you come to the realization that your life is not your own, you can better see why you should share your testimony. Everything that you've been though wasn't about you at all. It was about helping and being a blessing to someone else.

I had anticipated writing this book since 2002. Then, there it was—July 24 2011--and I finally decided, "I *have* to do this. So what if people find out more than I want them to know?" It's about pleasing God!

I asked God to quicken me with his spirit so that I could write and complete this book before the year was out. To help me get it done expeditiously because that lost time needed to be redeemed. Job 33:4: "The spirit of God has made me, and the breath of the almighty gives me life."

As a result of the experiences of my own life, I can testify today that God has use for, has great plans for—even glory for—a messed-up person who has experimented with drugs, who has been raped, who has been in the hospital due to mental stress, who's suffered child-growth-development problems after being molested, and endured physical abuse, mental abuse, verbal abuse, and child abuse.

This not a pity party. Please understand that mine is a testimony to how God can bring you out of any situation that you are in and use you for his glory. If, in fact, you have experienced any of these things that I've mentioned, praise God! This book is for you. I pray that the yoke of bondage be broken off your neck in the mighty matchless name of Jesus. The Lord specializes in the great outcomes. Matt 19:26: "But Jesus looked at them and said to them, with men this is impossible, but with God all things are possible."

3

Okay. Right about now, I know what you may be thinking: "Lord, I am not about to tell people my business," or "These things are too painful to talk about."

Well, the only thing I have to say to that is, "Stop being a man-pleaser."

That's right: a *man*-pleaser. Man doesn't have a hell or heaven to put you in. Come out of that cocoon and let the truth make you free. "Therefore, if the son makes you free, you shall be free indeed" (John 8:36).

I thank God for every trial and tribulation that came along, for each one made me strong. Each one came to make me whole. Most of all, they each gave me a testimony whereby I can share with others who may feel hopeless.

Oftentimes we wonder why we can't move forward. It's mainly because we won't let God use us for his glory. We already know he gets the glory out of everything, yet and still we ask, "What will people say?" We are ignorant to ask this question. We are blind and cannot see that God sees and knows all. At the same time, we seem to care more about what people will think rather than what God will, when it should be the other way around. "For they loved the praise of men more than the praise of God" (John 12:43).

We often get caught up with man because we need to feel accepted. Before you know it, we are people-driven. It's almost like being an addict—the addiction is the approval of other people. So, if you're wondering why you can't praise God, it could very well be because you are sitting on the throne yourself.

We are people-driven instead of purpose-driven.

Anna Marie McCutchen

Chapter 2: Blind Bartimaeus

I knew it was time to write this book. At the beginning of this year, 2011, I had the roughest start. And it didn't get any better. It was a really messy year for me.

The trials that I had endured were getting the best of me. It was hard for me to see how they could ever possibly work together for the good.

Before I knew it, I had gotten myself in lots of trouble. I confessed my ugly situation to the Lord. My question to God was, "How are you going to get me out of this mess?"

When I was in my quiet place, meditating, I could hear God speak to me. He let me know what I was going through. I was having a problem forgiving. I had been messed over by some folks whom I loved. I was unable to move past that problem.

The Lord reminded me of all the wrong *I* had done. Here's the catch: He showed me that I would be caught up if I didn't forgive because then I wouldn't be forgiven for my sins. Matthew 5:7: "Blessed are the merciful, for they shall obtain mercy."

This particular dilemma reminded me of the biblical story of blind Bartimaeus. Bartimaeus had a problem that seemed incapable of a solution.

My understanding of Blind Bartimaeus was enlightened the night I went to a church called the Church of Peace and Good Will to see Marvin Sapp perform. The Lord gave pastor

Sapp a word for the people that night. The word was "You've got to holler until he hears you."

Marvin Sapp began to explain the story of Bartimaeus, beginning with an etymological analysis of the man's name: The prefix "Bar" means "son of." The root, Timaeus, means "corrupt and filthy." So Bartimaeus is the son of a nasty, polluted man.

The story of blind Bartimaeus is in the Gospel of Mark, chapter 10:46-52: "And they came to Jericho, and, as he went out of Jericho with his disciples and a great number of people, blind Bartimaeus, the son of Timeus sat by the highway side, begging. And, when he heard that it was Jesus of Nazareth, he began to cry out and say, 'Jesus, thou son of David, have mercy on me'. And many charged him that he should hold his peace. But he cried the more a great deal, 'Thou son of David, have mercy on me.' And Jesus stood still and commanded him to be called. And they call the blind man, saying unto him, 'Be of good comfort; rise. He calls thee.' And he, casting away his garment, rose and came to Jesus. And Jesus answered and said unto him, "What wilt thou that I should do unto thee?' The blind man said unto him, 'Lord, that I might receive my sight.' And Jesus said unto him, 'Go thy way; thy faith hath made thee whole.' And immediately he received his sight and followed Jesus in the way."

You can clearly see from this story how it pleases God to take a situation that seems hopeless and impossible and breathe hopes and possibilities right on it. Job 6:8: "Oh that I might have my request and that God would grant me the thing that I long for!"

I admire the faith that blind Bartimaeus had. Notice how Jesus was moved by Bartimaeus's faith and thus restored his sight—and that Bartimaeus then followed Jesus in the way.

The story illustrated Mr. Sapp's point—that we need to holler until God hears us. Forget about what people around you are saying. No matter what type of obstacle or hindrance blocks your way, no matter traumatic occurrences you have experienced, you can make it. God sees the good that is in you. The steps of a good man are ordered by the Lord, and he delighteth in his way. Though he fall, he shall not be utterly cast down. For the Lord upholdeth him with his hand" (Psalm 37:23-24).

We need to step out of our comfort zone to a place where God can process us. We have to forget about what people might think when we holler for God's help. When I holler, it is a desperate cry . I'm hollering, "Lord Jesus, help me get out of this mess that I'm in." As far as people are concerned, if I could get what I needed from them, I wouldn't have to holler for Jesus.

Don't be afraid or embarrassed to ask the Lord for help. Steven Furtick once said, "Walking in bold faith takes confidence. But

11

healthy confidence is born out of genuine humility. The two must work in tandem. Confidence without humility is arrogance. Humility without confidence is weakness. They're both biblical essentials for a life of true faith."

Having faith for a breakthrough doesn't come from what you see; it comes from what you hear. Hebrews 11:1: "Now faith is the substance of things hoped for, the evidence of things not seen." Bartimaeus didn't see Jesus, but he heard him. He sensed the power.

Bartimaeus had a desperate need and assumed the wailing, abject position of a beggar. Many of us, on the other hand, have a desperate need but don't have the right posture. God is checking out our posture. Unlike Bartimaeus, we can't get our breakthrough because we don't want to look odd or awkward or strange to people.

Bartimaeus's behavior and position looked strange to the people around him ("many charged him that he should hold his peace"), but he was in the right posture for God. His request wasn't a casual prayer but a desperate cry.

To be delivered from all our fears, we must remember to render our desperate cries to the Lord and not think of how we look to other people. "I sought the Lord, and he heard me, and delivered me from all my fears" (Psalms 34:4). When we set our affection on the Lord and the things that are above, the mess that people conjure up will become a small thing. When we stop worrying about who's judging us, who's looking at us askance, who's hating us, we can really get the blessing. This is when you decide nothing can separate you from his love. Romans 8:35-39: "Who shall separate us from the love of Christ? Shall tribulation or distress or persecution or famine or nakedness or peril or sword? As it is written, we are accounted as sheep for the slaughter. Nay, in all these things we are more than conquerors through Him that loves us. For I am persuaded that neither death nor life nor angels nor principalities nor powers nor things present nor things to come nor the height nor the depth, nor any other creature shall be able to separate us from the love of God, which is in Christ Jesus our Lord."

DON'T HATE ON YOUR HATERS

Anna Marie McCutchen

Chapter 3: Don't Hate on Your Haters

How do you think you have made it this far? Bet you thought it was because you are so wise. Or maybe because you have been empowered with some sort of supernatural strength. Wrong. The grace of God. brought you this far. No, you didn't deserve it; it was unearned; it was unmerited kindness on the part of God. The mercy and forgiveness of God has brought you this far.

As odd as this may sound, your haters also helped you. Everything that people have done against you in life, God turned it around for your good. Romans 8:28: "And we know that all things work together for good to them that love God, to them who are the called according to his purpose." We need these types of people in our lives to push us to the heights of which we are now elevated. To places we are intended to go and to grow. We should send our haters a postcard thanking them for all their assistance, because, without their help, we would never strive or thrive.

We need to recognize that even the devil's steps are ordered by the Lord. He can do no more than God allows. The devil, our haters— they're all part of God's grand plan to help us step out of our comfort zone in order to get something from him. He puts the haters on a divine assignment, then in turn takes us to our divine appointment.

God wouldn't have to shake us up like that if we would just open up to his will.

Unfortunately, we are, in most cases, hostile to his will; we're closed and in control. That's why we need haters to come along and cause trouble that will press us and shake us into alignment with God's will. If we would just open up, God wouldn't have to assign so many haters to our life.

Again, we must remember to love our haters. God created them. He still gets glory out of all things. That is why they are on divine assignment because God is using them to bring the best out of us. I Peter 1:7: "That the trial of your faith, being much more precious than of gold that perisheth, though it be tried with fire, might be found unto praise and honor and glory at the appearing of Jesus Christ."

Our former pastor, Claude Allen, used to teach us that we should give thanks in all things. Not that we would appreciate all things because all things aren't always good. However, we need to anticipate a good outcome. Pastor

Claude would teach us that we need a positive mindset. He said we should look at circumstances and say, "Well Lord there must be a blessing in it."

Looking at complicated circumstances puts me in the mind of a kaleidoscope. It's like looking into a lens and seeing things one way, but, when you continue to look further, you see how circumstances change.

This is how we should look at negative people—people through whom the enemy works: think of them like the kaleidoscope. First, you look and say, "Looks like the devil is using this hater or these haters to bring me down." Then you can adjust your lens and notice how these haters are working in God's favor for you. Because they are on divine assignment, there is a blessing to be found in their hatred.

So remember your motivator (God). Your enemies strengthen you, make you better, and take you further. If "no weapon that is formed against thee shall prosper" (Isaiah 54:17), then haters can't be more than a blessing in the making.

Anna Marie McCutchen

Chapter 4: Short-term Pain, Long-time Gain

Just as we're not too crazy about a work-out exercise, we don't like any painful process. But there's a saying: "You can only get out what you put in."

Remember, for example, when you were growing up and were mischievous and needed the belt. Your parents would say, "This is hurting me just as much as it is hurting you; you will appreciate it in the long run." You probably didn't think so back then.

If I had to give an opinion about my childhood and growth experience, I would have to say that it was pretty rough. Some of the things that I went through really messed me up. I sometimes thought that no one else in the world could be experiencing the kind of nonsense that I was dealing with.

I would sometimes sit up all night wondering why I had to suffer so much at such a young age. There were times I would go to bed with hunger pains. Other nights I didn't sleep at all because my punishment had been so severe. It was hard to rest, sometimes, when my head was bleeding from being hit with a book or a cast-iron skillet. I tried reasoning with myself: *Maybe I am just a really bad little girl.*

It was painful for me to hear my mother tell me that I wouldn't probably live to see 21. Wasn't easy hearing statements like,. "You'll probably get pregnant and be a high school dropout." The verbal abuse was worse than the physical abuse. But those statements caused me to make it my priority to ensure that each and every one of those remarks was a lie from the pit. Looking on the bright side of the scope, I could see how this messed-up situation worked in God's favor, simply by making a liar out of the devil. I had the victory over negativity.

I'm not telling you this so that you will feel sorry for me—or so I can wallow in my own self-pity. On the contrary, I'm trying to illustrate how pain and suffering can make you become a better you—when you realize that it's part of God's plan to test you, to make you stronger, to get you to lean on him.

Who would have thought I would be able to appreciate how messed up things were for me, having been abused as a child, neglected, more deprived than any of my peers, and so on and so forth. Now that I am older, I can truly say that it was good that I was afflicted. Psalm 119:71: "It is good for me that I have been afflicted, that I might learn thy statutes."

Chapter 5: My Mess

I think that it is absolutely amazing what God can do inside of something that is weak, frail, inconsistent, foolish, and a number of other things. God can be sure to get the glory when he uses people like this because they recognize the glory is of him and not of them.

Looking back on all of my past mistakes, shortcomings, weaknesses, and so forth, I never thought I would even live long enough to put it all in a book.

When I was in grade school, I may have had a case of ADHD or bipolar mood disorder (BMD)—or possibly both. I was never diagnosed with it at that time, but I certainly had enough symptoms. I say that because I would always act out in class and end up in trouble. For one, I was acting out of pain and disappointment. For two, I was more deprived than any of the kids with whom I came in contact. And, for three, I knew that when I got home I would have no freedom to go outside or play with any of those other kids on the block.

Back then, my mother, Carolyn, was overprotective and quite paranoid. Today, my mother is quite paranoid, which is understandable because she has a case of schizophrenia.

The things that I went through as a child had an effect on me then, and have a continuing effect on me, even now.

I really thank God for the hardships that I faced because they taught me to persevere in life. Unlike a lot of other children, I lacked the necessities in life. My parents were not to blame because they did the best they knew how to do.

My father, Junior McCutchen, was a truck driver most of his life until he got injured on the job. He really couldn't deal with the fact that he couldn't provide for his family the way that he wanted to. As a result, he turned to drinking. He would drink excessively because he couldn't cope with the realities of life. My father passed when I was around twenty years old. His death didn't make me a better person—I got worse.

In the year following my father's death, I probably did everything there was to do under the sun, from clubbing to experimenting with drugs, stealing from department stores, and dating a man old enough to be my father while having another man on the side—a drug dealer who was trying to teach me how to sell marijuana. I may have been mischievous before my father died, but, afterward, I was *bad*.

I knew that I was going to die if I didn't get a handle on life. I mentioned to you earlier that my mother would always say that I'd be dead by 21. Ironically, at that age, I was living every day like it was my last. Not in a saved way but in a sinner's way. Proverbs 14:12: "There is a way that seems right unto a man but the end thereof are the ways of death." I prayed to God that he would do a quick work in me. Romans 8:11: "But if the spirit of him that raised up Jesus from the dead dwell in you, he that raised up Christ from the dead shall also quicken your mortal bodies by his spirit that dwells in you."

God is a prayer answering God. He delivered me from death and from being sin sick. I was literally sin sick from doing all the wrong things. It was hurting my family, my body, and my future. I was sick of the sin that I was in and ready to shout to God to relieve, just as blind Bartimaeus cried aloud with a desperate cry.

I hope you understand now that, sometimes, if you let people stop you from getting your prayer through or your breakthrough, it can cost you your life. In my case—as in Bartimaeus's—God was faithful to answer. Although things got worse before they got better, God knew what his plans were for me. Jeremiah 29:11: "For I know the thoughts that I think toward you, says the Lord, thoughts of peace, and not of evil, to give you an expected end." No one said it better than Marvin Sapp: "He saw the best in me, when everyone else around could only see the worst in me."

Anna Marie McCutchen

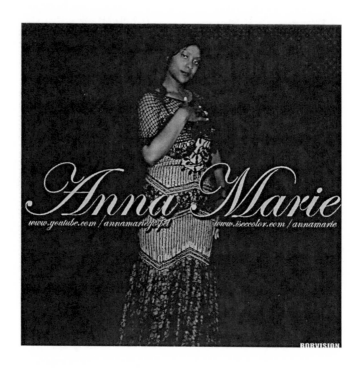

Chapter 6: From the Heart

Who am I to God? Can God really love someone like me with all of my imperfections? Why have I been through so much? Can I truly please God? Will my good outweigh my bad? Can I make it to heaven? These are some of the questions that I often find myself asking God. Maybe I shouldn't question God, but these questions are important, and I can't help but ponder them every day.

It's really difficult to know where you stand with the Lord when you examine yourself. The bible has declared that you will fall short of God's glory. In this case, you have only God's grace to depend on.

One thing that I realized is that, if you favor his righteous cause, he will preserve your life. For example, I write, sing, and promote Gospel music every day. This is the gift that God has bestowed on me. His intention is for me to utilize the gifts. In doing so, it helps spread the gospel message and puts me in the favor of his righteous cause. Psalm 35:27: "Let them shout for joy, and be glad, that favor my righteous cause. Let them say continually, 'Let the Lord be magnified, which hath pleasure in the prosperity of his servant.'"

Before I was developed to do his good pleasure, I had to go through a lot of mess. No one said it better than the great Bishop Jakes: "You don't know the story behind the glory. Some kind of way trouble was a friend of mind because it had a way of putting fire under my feet, and I would run for my life. People ask me all the time, 'How did you get the hope that lies in you? What makes you strive the way you do?' All I can tell them is, 'If you know where I came from, then you would be able to appreciate where I'm trying to go.'"

That's why I can hardly understand why people look at some of the things that others are doing and say, "That should be me." They have no idea of the weight and responsibility that comes with certain tasks. I tell people all of the time, "Don't think you want any of this because you almost have to take a death walk to get it." Joyce Myers said it once in one of her messages: "If you want to get where I am, you have to first go where I've been."

Since this is from the heart, I can mention today's date. October 16, 2011. The time is 8:30 p.m. Two things took place that really touched my heart. First, I had to sing at the Henderson Memorial United Methodist Church where my cousin Wendell Davis was a member for more than 47 years. This was not just an ordinary service; it was considered a memorial service for my cousin, and we are still celebrating the life of Wendell Norman Davis. On this night, they also acknowledged that he was the founder of the annual jubilee ceremony in 1983, which brings us to the 28th annual celebration this year. I was thankful when they opened the platform to anyone who had thoughts they wanted to express.

This was my opportunity to share with everyone about cousin Wendell—to explain what a great mentor he had been to me, and how much his mentorship has affected my life. Wendell's ministry was inspiring. He had a pure, transcending heart.

I remember him putting the fear of God in me when I was five years old. He said, "If you don't use those gifts God gave you, he is going to spank you really good." I admired his charisma and respected everything that he had to say. At that time, he was teaching at Cass Technical High school. So, every time he would visit, I would be just as attentive as I would be in a classroom. The one thing that he taught me was that, if God has need of you and you let him use you, he will preserve your life and sustain you for what he needs you for.

I thank God for the calling. I thank him for the increase. Praise God for jubilee that represents increase. Leviticus 26:4: "the land shall yield her increase."

The second thing that happened that night hurt me emotionally. I called to wish a happy birthday in advance to Kenneth Riggs, an old friend, an older guy I used to date in high school—only to find out that he had passed away a few days before. His sister Marcia answered his phone and said he died Oct 13.

No one like to get news like this But one thing I do know is that Kenneth no longer has to suffer all the afflictions that he put up with for years. I will always remember how he cared for my father when my father was alive. My father had to go back and forth for radiation treatment when he had cancer. Riggs was kind enough to let me drive one of his new cars so I could take my father for treatments and go to and from high school. May the Lord allow his soul to rest in peace. I Thessalonians 5:23: "And the very God of peace sanctify you wholly; and I pray God your whole spirit and soul and body be preserved, blameless until the coming of our Lord Jesus Christ."

Chapter 7: The Message

There's no more time for procrastinating. It's time for you to tell your story. The bible declares that our life is a story that people read. 2 Corinthians 3:2: "Ye are our epistle written in our hearts, known and read of all men."

"Why," you might ask, "would I tell my story? What is this message stuff all about?"

I'll tell you what it's all about. It's about God getting the glory out of your life. It's about people being delivered from your message and your testimony. People are empowered when they know you've been on the rough side of the mountain and yet came out victorious. It brings a sense of hope to one's self.

Would you rather be a hopeless person with no purpose? That would mean that you're living is in vain. It would mean that there's no message coming from your life that could bless anyone else. That certainly isn't the case. If it were, God would not have had a need to create you at all. It's a matter of you letting him use you as a vessel. Let him use you as a message. Yes, I know it's easier taking a back seat in life than it is to be put on the front line. However it's better to die empty, having fulfilled everything you were sent to do in life.

People would often tell me they saw greatness in me. I would say to myself, "Yeah, right. You must need your eyes checked because I have too many issues for greatness." Later I realized that God placed those people in my life to speak the words of faith that would get me focused.

I have to be honest. There is no greater investment in life than in being a people builder. Just look at some of the great leaders who went before us—Martin Luther King, John F. Kennedy, Malcolm X, Rosa Parks, etc. These were great leaders who had the power to change a nation. And there were other trailblazers who went before them with great messages that they could build from.

God always uses one to move a multitude. You never know what you could be building. You could very well be building a nation by making a positive impact on one individual. In turn, that one individual could change a nation. With this in mind, it could be easier than you think to change the world.

I know you've heard this saying before: "If you want to change the world, then consider changing yourself." Michael Jackson said it better: "I'm looking at the man in the mirror and asking him to change his ways." He made it clear; Mr. Jackson said himself that no message could be made any clearer. It really doesn't' take a genius to know this. Change one person, and you might change the world. Change yourself, for you might be that one person.

We have absolutely too many people in this world who are a part of all the problems. We hardly have any who are willing to be the solution. It makes sense to see that people who talk don't do it, and people who do don't talk. It's easier to talk and complain about problems than it is to solve a problem. Most people choose what they think is the easier route (complaining, not solving). Believe it or not, it's actually easier to take on the hard task. Lining up with destiny puts you on a much smoother path.

For instance, consider the story of Pharaoh. In Exodus, God puts Moses on divine assignment. He tells Moses to "return into Egypt [and] see that thou do all these wonders before Pharaoh, which I have put in your hand: but I will harden his heart, that he shall not let the people go, and you shall say unto Pharaoh, 'Thus says the Lord: Israel is my son, even my first born, and I say unto thee, "Let my son go, that he may serve me: and, if you refuse to let him go, behold—I will slay your son, even your first born"'" (Exodus 4:21-23).

The Lord purposely arranged for Pharaoh to operate out of disobedience at the same time he warned him of all the hardships that he would face for disobeying. Everything that God said came to pass, and Pharaoh suffered great hardships from having a hard heart.

All of these things teach us and provide us with spiritual ammunition. God gives us a message. He expects us to learn from other people's mistakes.

We get the message on how smooth our life can be by following the path of obedience when we study Genesis 22, in which. Abraham is commanded by the Lord to offer up his only son as a sacrifice. I know this must have been hard for Abraham, but the bible says that Abraham staggered not at the promise of God. "And Abraham stretched forth his hand and took the knife to slay his son, and the angel of the Lord called unto him out of heaven and said 'Abraham, Abraham,' and he said, 'Here I am.' 'Lay not your hand upon the lad, neither do thou anything unto him, for I now know that you fear God, seeing thou has not withheld thy son, your only son from me.' And Abraham lifted up his eyes and looked and beheld behind him a ram caught in the thicket by his horns; and Abraham went and took the ram and offered him up for a burnt offering instead of his son.

"So Abraham called that place 'The Lord Will Provide.' And to this day it is said, 'On the mountain of the Lord it will be provided.'

"The angel of the Lord called to Abraham from heaven a second time and said, '"I swear by myself," declares the Lord, "that, because you have done this and have not withheld your son, your only son, I will surely bless you and make your descendants as numerous as the stars in the sky and as the sand on the seashore. Your descendants will take possession of the cities of their enemies, and through your offspring all nations on earth will be blessed, because you have obeyed me"'" (Genesis 22: 10-18).

I'll stop here; I just need to praise God right here, thank God for his wondrous works. The message here is, if you believe God, he can make a way out of no way. Abraham believed God, and it was counted unto him for righteousness.

Several verses of this scriptural story touched me most: "Isaac spoke unto Abraham his father and said, 'My father,' and he said, 'Here I am, my son.' And he said, 'Behold the fire and the wood, but where is the lamb for a burnt offering?'

"And Abraham said, 'My son, God will provide himself a lamb for a burnt offering.' So they went both of them together. And they came to the place which God had told him of; and Abraham built an altar there, and laid the wood in order, and bound Isaac his son, and laid him on the altar upon the wood" (Genesis 22: 7-9).

Although Abraham couldn't bear to tell his son Isaac that he was the sacrifice, he still proceeded in obedience to God. Notice that, while Isaac was being bound by his father, he didn't ask any more questions. This message of faith is one of the greatest in history. We learn through Abraham how God honors faith. There is always a ram in the bush for the believers.

"Okay," you're asking yourself, "where is she going with all of this?" I've told you already. It's the message. There is a message emanating from your life that God wants to use in order to bless someone else. Whether it's a book, a song, an explanation, or something else, that's for you to discover. You have to be obedient to whatever it is. *I'm telling you!!*

I know this may not be the best book you have ever read. I wasn't looking for a best seller. I was aiming to please God. *I'm telling you!!*

I wasn't sure how I could make this book a reality, but I placed my faith in God, and here it is. I didn't think I could manage to arrange for its publication. It was a move of God. He said that, if I had enough faith to follow through, then he would find a way for me. That's why I knew he was moving me to write this book.

Okay. Let's get back to the point. When we look at the gospel message of Jesus Christ, we understand that he came through 42 generations to bring us the gospel of peace. Ephesians 6:15: "And your feet shod with the preparation of the gospel of peace"; I Corinthians 14:33: "For God is not a God of disorder but of peace—as in all the congregations of the Lord's people."

Jesus Christ, who was without sin, was born to die for our sins, thus reconciling us with God. Isaiah 53:5: "But he was pierced for our transgressions, he was crushed for our iniquities; the punishment that brought us peace was on him, and by his wounds we are healed."

Where would we be if Jesus hadn't fulfilled his purpose in our lives? We would be without hope if Jesus had not been obedient to the father. Philippians 2:8: "And being found in appearance as a man, he humbled himself by becoming obedient unto death— even death on a cross!" Jesus's followers bear his image. They bring the message of reconciliation to others, urging them to accept God's peace through faith.

You can certainly find evidence in the bible that God uses us as examples for others. See, for instance, II Corinthians 5:18-20: "All this is from God, who reconciled us to himself through Christ and gave us the ministry of reconciliation; that God was reconciling the world to himself in Christ, not counting people's sins against them. And he has committed to us the message of reconciliation. We are therefore Christ's ambassadors, as though God were making his appeal through us. We implore you on Christ's behalf: Be reconciled to God."

Like Christ, we can make a world of difference when we fulfill his divine will for us. So what is the thing that you think you can't do? What is the thing that people have said you can't do? For me it was writing books. That turned out to be the very thing God said I *can* do. So just remember that your doubt could be holding up your destiny. Discover your purpose. Pursue your goals. Let us, like Christ, accomplish what we were sent and meant to do in life. Give your message.

Chapter 8: Movement

The very first thing that the book of Genesis teaches us about God's spirit is that it moves. Genesis 1:1-2: "In the beginning God created the heaven and the earth. And the earth was without form, and void; and darkness was upon the face of the deep. And the spirit of God moved upon the face of the waters."

Throughout the entire bible, from Genesis to Revelation, God's movement is expressed. Our great God moved all the minor and major prophets in the old testament to perform a particular task.

It's no wonder that God considers mankind his greatest creation. God isn't just moving and visiting us for a particular task anymore. Now that we've been baptized in Jesus's name and received the precious gift of the Holy Ghost, Christ lives in us. Colossians 1:25-27: "Whereof I am made a minister, according to the dispensation of God which is given to me for you, to fulfill the word of God; Even the mystery which hath been hid from ages and from generations, but now is made manifest to his saints: To whom God would make known what is the riches of the glory of this mystery among the Gentiles; which is Christ in you, the hope of glory:" Through these verses, we should understand how important it is that we let God move us. When we get in the movement of God, we can operate in the supernatural. I admit this is not easy—because of our flesh that gets in the way. Our flesh, which is enmity or an enemy of the cross, tends to stand in the way sometimes. The thoughts we think don't always line up with God. Isaiah 55:8: "For my thoughts are not your thoughts, neither are your ways my ways, saith the Lord"—which is God's polite way of telling us that our brains can be inferior and sinful.

Isaiah 55:9: "For as the heavens are higher than the earth, so are my ways higher than your ways, and my thoughts than your thoughts"— which is God's not-so-polite way of suggesting that our flesh is hostile to the Lord's will.

We are contrary to the will of God because our heart and mind are not in the right place. For this reason, we must mortify the deeds of the flesh with much prayer and fasting. which enables us to be more sensitive to the will of the Father. When we are more in the spirit, we can tell our flesh what to do instead of having our flesh control us: "Casting down imaginations, and every high thing that exalteth itself against the knowledge of God, and bringing into captivity every thought to the obedience of Christ" (. 2 Corinth 10:5)

It's hard to be time sensitive if we're not spiritually in tune to what God is saying. Just imagine: suppose it's your season but you aren't aware of it! You could be somewhere doing the wrong thing at the right time.

It could also be the other way around. It could *not* be your season, and you might be doing the right things at the wrong time. I have had this experience more than once and can tell you that it's really not a good feeling. It leaves you feeling twisted and tired because you're not spiritually in tune with God.

Allow me to elaborate. I would almost have to go verbatim to explain a powerful sermon taught by Bishop T.D. Jakes on the wisdom of the locust. I feel that it's very necessary to talk about the locust because the locust has some attributes that we as saints of God should have.

The locust is a straight-winged insect that resembles the grasshopper. His wings are narrow. The locust can travel through the air for more than 2,000 miles at a time. But the locust's real strength isn't in his wings; it's in his legs. He can jump 200 times his height. But notice what's more powerful than how far he travels or how high he can jump: he knows *when* to jump. He has wisdom about how to deal with the wind.

Well, what is the wind? The bible says the wind is like God's spirit. John 3:8: "The wind bloweth where it listeth, and thou hearest the sound thereof, but canst not tell whence it cometh, and whither it goeth: so is every one that is born of the Spirit."

The locust is so smart that he waits for a gust of wind to blow, then propels himself into the currents of the wind. When he is in the wind, he is not able to chart his own course but is dependent on the navigation of the wind. Wherever the wind blows, that's where the locust goes. There is no way the locust could travel for miles the way it does without the mighty rushing of the wind. He travels without struggle or stress because of the power of the wind.

Recognize the wind. We all have strengths and weaknesses. And, like the locusts, we can learn how to operate life from the position of our strength rather than our weakness. The locust's wings are narrow, but his strength is in his legs. He knows when to jump and is able to jump high. Jesus is our navigation system; when we are spiritually in tune, he can direct our path. Jeremiah 10:23: "O Lord, I know that the way of man is not in himself: it is not in man that walketh to direct his steps."

We as human beings need to recognize the wind of God. When the wind is blowing in our lives, that is our window of opportunity. The wind of God is able to blow us out of the situation that we may be in. The wind of God can blow us into financial blessings, favor, and success. It can blow us away from sin, fear, doubt, bondage, and strongholds. We should be praying: "God, blow on my life, my family, my health, and my finances. In the mighty name of Jesus, blow over my ministry and the calling and purpose you have over my life In Jesus's name, I want to recognize God's wind. I want to experience the effects of where the wind is taking me."

About five years ago I was in the wind of God. I took a leap of faith, and God blew me into Atlanta, Georgia, where I began recording Gospel music. It was a supernatural experience. I knew it was a move of God because, if I were operating in the natural world, I wouldn't have been able to make sense out of it. My co-worker, Keesha Macon, almost discouraged me not to take the chance I was taking. She just couldn't see why I would take my last check for the summer and spend it on a plane ticket to and hotel room in Atlanta at the time, we were both public-safety officers in the Detroit Public Schools. Both she and I were ten-month employees without any income over the summer. She said, "Anna, you have got to be out of your mind." What she didn't understand was that I was trying to be. I had been concentrating, praying for the mind of Christ and looking for a move of God.

I Corinth 2:12-16: "Now we have received, not the spirit of the world, but the spirit which is of God; that we might know the things that are freely given to us of God. Which things also we speak, not in the words which man's wisdom teacheth, but which the Holy Ghost teacheth; comparing spiritual things with spiritual. But the natural man receiveth not the things of the Spirit of God: for they are foolishness unto him:

neither can he know them, because they are spiritually discerned. But he that is spiritual judgeth all things, yet he himself is judged of no man. For who hath known the mind of the Lord, that he may instruct him? but we have the mind of Christ."

Philippians 2:5: "Let this mind be in you, which was also in Christ Jesus:"

When you are being blessed to operate supernaturally, you cannot confer with the flesh. If I hadn't trusted in the Lord, I would be in a world of trouble after being laid off by the school board. I would never have received God's supernatural providence had I listened to man. I thank God for the wind that I was in. Psalm 118:8: "It is better to trust in the Lord than to put confidence in man."

All I'm saying is this: Remember the message from the locusts." The message is, "Don't give up." Stay focused. When the wind of God blows over your life, jump into your destiny and see the mighty hand of God move in your life.

Chapter 9: Heart Condition

Do you have a heart condition? This is something that you should take the time to consider. My answer would be yes. We all do. The bible says that the heart is deceitful. Jeremiah 17:9: "The heart is deceitful above all things, and desperately wicked: who can know it?"

Sometimes we think we are sweet. Are we? We should constantly check ourselves to avoid self-deception. Half the time we are bittersweet. If we had a pure heart, we would be flowing along with God's will. But, if God has to constantly tug at our hearts to get us to do something, it should bother our conscience. Our heart and mind are connected—and this is where the heart condition comes in to play.

We need to thank the Lord because he is great and renews us day by day. II Corinthians 4:15-16: "For all things are for your sakes, that the abundant grace might through the thanksgiving of many redound to the glory of God. For which cause we faint not; but, though our outward man perish, yet the inward man is renewed day by day." The Lord loves us so much that he strives with us until our hearts and minds come in alignment with his calling and purpose for our lives.

God will not always strive with man. We know that sin is death, but obedience to God can lengthen our days. Genesis 6:3: "And the Lord said, "My spirit will not always strive with man, for that he also is flesh: yet his days shall be a hundred and twenty years."

We are so often closed up to God's will. There is a struggle that's going on. I remember plenty of times in my life where God would send pressings and shakings until I opened up to his will. God wouldn't have had to shake me so hard if I would have just gone in the direction that he was sending me. Oh, yeah, we get the message from the Lord about what to do, but we do the contrary because of that heart condition of ours.

After the Lord has to almost beat us up in the spirit, we find ourselves crying with tears running down our face. After God has delivered us so many times already, we, like the Israelites, try for deliverance again. God wants to accept us. So all of our lives he strives with us because of our hearts. He wants us to get our mind right. Psalm 19:14: "Let the words of my mouth, and the meditation of my heart, be acceptable in thy sight, O Lord, my strength, and my redeemer."

God doesn't want us to play hard to get with him. In truth, we need him more than he needs us. If the Lord were to stop striving with us, the enemy would swallow us up. Hebrews 3:15: "While it is said, 'Today, if ye will hear his voice, harden not your hearts, as in the provocation.'" God strives with us for the anointing that he is calling forth. He is all knowing. He knows that you have to suffer and endure hardships before the real anointing comes. II Timothy 2:12: "If we suffer, we shall also reign with him; if we deny him, he also will deny us." The Lord is preparing us. He's conditioning us for what is ahead.

PROPHETIC MESSAGE

Anna Marie McCutchen

Chapter 10: Prophetic Messages

In this last chapter, I would like to record some of the prophecies that have been spoken by different individuals whom God placed in my path. It's important that these messages be implemented. For what I have been trying to express through the book is that we are all God's messengers in one way or another.

God is so good that he allowed me to rediscover my notebook—the one I thought I had lost, the one in which I recorded these prophecies. What a serendipitous coincidence this was. Praise God! I would have ended at chapter nine had I not found the notebook, so it was confirmation—confirmation of God's love, confirmation of the fact that he had guided me to write this book, confirmation that there was a further reason for this book to exist.

March 24, 2009. I was at a gas station. A young man told me, "I will support your music." I thanked him. Then, out of nowhere, he added, "God is going to bless you."

A preacher spoke at the Pentecostal Church of Jesus Christ (PCJC) a few years ago. I can't remember his name or very much else about him—only that he was a white man and only what he prophesied for me. He pointed at me and told me in front of the whole congregation, "When you come, you bring God's presence. You have a praise inside of you that is able to burn up everything that is going on around you. The business God is giving you is *big*."

I remember when I was a member at Jesus Tabernacle (JTDM). One of the saints walked up to me and advised, "Get ready because you are going to blow up."

Another time at JTDM, a married couple who went on to be pastors prophesied that God is going to bless me in a really big way. I received it right then and there. But I asked them how they knew. Pastor Bullock answered "God showed me and told me to tell you. And, when God tells me something, I have to be obedient."

I was asking a question in bible class one night at JTDM. Before the question was answered, Pastor David Billy pronounced to me that I had had a revelation.

First lady Elaine Billy prayed for me once. She began to yell out of her mouth that I was a mighty woman of God and that doors were going to open.

When I visited Global Destiny in Duluth, Georgia, a few people there spoke into my life.

First a minister named Eric Meriwether told me that he saw God blessing me with supernatural finances. Another minister at Global Destiny told me that everything about me was for the glory of God. Robert Sims, my prophetic friend from Atlanta, told me that I had power that I hadn't even used yet. He even assisted me by introducing me to two well-established music producers in the Atlanta area, with whom I was able to begin recording gospel music.

Elder Elderby from PCJC told me that, as long as I keep God before me, God will bless me everywhere I go—even all over the world.

Minister Rollin, from PCJC, told me that I have no clue what the Lord wants to do with me. He even began to pray the spirit of humility over me.

Our former pastor Claude Allen Jr. told me that he was waiting to see me reach my full potential.

Prophetess Carmen Jones from JTDM told me that God was going to bless me 1000 fold.

Sister Stephanie, who is like a spiritual mother to me, said that God would perform mighty exploits through me.

I gave Marvine Allen's daughter one of my gospel CDs at PCJC. She pointed to me and said, "You are a very prosperous woman."

Last, but not least our new pastor of PCJC, Elder Keith L. Spiller, prophesied to me in the year of 2010. He said that I was definitely going higher. He even said that I can do anything I set my mind to do because I am one of life's go-getters.

There have been countless other prophecies spoken to me in my life. These are just a few that have been recorded. We know that every good—that any perfect thing—comes from the

Lord. I personally know that these prophetic messages helped to increase my faith. Some things have already come to pass, and others I am contemplating.

The bible says that we should write our vision and make it plain. Habakkuk 2:2: "Write the vision and makes it plain upon tables that he may run that reads it."

This is my vision. I have written it. I hope I have made it plain to you. I hope that you will do as I have done, and run with it!

Let Us Pray

Father God, in the mighty name of Jesus, we come as humbly as we know how. Asking you to forgive us for anything that we may have said or done, or anything we didn't do that may have caused you to be displeased. We thank you for hearing our prayers. We thank you in advance for forgiveness. Thank you for bringing more insight to us. Continue to give us the wisdom, knowledge, and understanding that we need. Order our steps and direct our path. Squeeze every single drop of glory out of our lives. We plead by the blood of Jesus. We bind any hindering spirits that would come against the will of God for our lives. Bless us to be a message for Christ's sake. Now, father, we decree and declare it to be so! In the mighty matchless name of Jesus Christ. And the believer said, "Amen."

Acknowledgements

To my producer, Walt E. Nelson, who is also a mentor, thank you for speaking the words of faith. Walt was reading a book in July of 2011 entitled *God Is My CEO* by Larry Julian. I asked him how the book was, and he said it was pretty good. He pointed to me and said, "I'm ready to read *your* book." That helped to increase my faith in myself—in my ability to actually accomplish this task. Thanks, Walt, for believing in me.

I would also like to thank Randall Jarrett, who is a prayer warrior.

Thank you, Paula Smith, for telling me that there is greatness in me. Thanks even more for having my back in Murray Wright when we were in Public Safety.

To Bishops David and Elaine Billy who kept me on a fast.

To Rodger Cozart, who had a positive influence on me;. he told me to always dress for success.

To Toriana Dismuke, who told me to guard my anointing.

To Faye Brandon, who aided in my back-and-forth to the airport when I traveled to Atlanta to record. You were faithful when it was below zero. Even at 3:00 in the morning, you didn't hesitate on the mission. Praise God.

Special thanks to Mr. and Mrs. Morbley, who let me reside in their beautiful home when I went to Charlotte, North Carolina. Thanks for your mentorship and for making me build my website.

Special Thanks to Bobby Jones, Trinity Broadcast Network, tv Channel 33, tv Channel 38 (the Word Network), AM radio stations 1440 and 1340, FM radio station 103.5, and all of the other television and radio stations who allowed me to be a part of their Gospel programming.

Also Tekiendra Batts. Special thanks to Ke-ke. I really admire you. Not just because you were the valedictorian of our class, but because you never hesitated to tell me what would benefit me. When I went to Wayne State, you warned me that declaring a major in some field that you really don't want to be in is *not* a good goal in life. "Make an investment that will work for you." Thanks, Ke-ke, for keeping it real.

Anna Marie McCutchen

Journal

I admonish you to use this journal as a personal tool of reference. Reflect on where God has brought you from and discover where he is taking you.

Anna Marie McCutchen

Mess

_____

_____

_____

_____

_____

_____

_____

_____

_____

_____

_____

_____

_____

_____

_____

_____

_____

_____

_____

_____

Message

_____

_____

_____

_____

_____

_____

_____

_____

_____

_____

_____

_____

_____

_____

_____

_____

_____

_____

_____

_____

_____

_____

_____

_____

_____

_____

_____

Anna Marie McCutchen

Mess

Message

_____

_____

_____

_____

_____

_____

_____

_____

_____

_____

_____

_____

_____

_____

_____

_____

_____

_____

_____

_____

_____

_____

_____

_____

_____

_____

Anna Marie McCutchen

Mess

Message

_____

_____

_____

_____

_____

_____

_____

_____

_____

_____

_____

_____

_____

_____

_____

_____

_____

_____

_____

_____

_____

_____

_____

_____

_____

_____

_____

Anna Marie McCutchen

Mess

_____
_____
_____
_____
_____
_____
_____
_____
_____
_____
_____
_____
_____
_____
_____
_____
_____
_____
_____
_____
_____
_____
_____
_____
_____
_____
_____

Message

_____

_____

_____

_____

_____

_____

_____

_____

_____

_____

_____

_____

_____

_____

_____

_____

_____

_____

_____

_____

_____

_____

_____

_____

_____

_____

_____

_____

Anna Marie McCutchen

Mess

Message

_____
_____
_____
_____
_____
_____
_____
_____
_____
_____
_____
_____
_____
_____
_____
_____
_____
_____
_____
_____
_____
_____
_____
_____
_____

Anna Marie McCutchen

Mess

Message

_____

_____

_____

_____

_____

_____

_____

_____

_____

_____

_____

_____

_____

_____

_____

_____

_____

_____

_____

_____

_____

_____

_____

_____

_____

_____

_____

_____

Anna Marie McCutchen

Mess

Message

_____
_____
_____
_____
_____
_____
_____
_____
_____
_____
_____
_____
_____
_____
_____
_____
_____
_____
_____
_____
_____
_____
_____
_____
_____
_____
_____
_____

Anna Marie McCutchen

Mess

Message

_____

_____

_____

_____

_____

_____

_____

_____

_____

_____

_____

_____

_____

_____

_____

_____

_____

_____

_____

_____

_____

_____

_____

_____

_____

_____

_____

Anna Marie McCutchen

Mess

Message

_____

_____

_____

_____

_____

_____

_____

_____

_____

_____

_____

_____

_____

_____

_____

_____

_____

_____

_____

_____

_____

_____

_____

_____

_____

_____

_____

_____

CPSIA information can be obtained
at www.ICGtesting.com
Printed in the USA
FFOW01n1803280415
13010FF